RAY PRICE

BIOGRAPHY

The Lasting Legacy of a Country Legend
– How His Music Still Lives On

TOM M. TRAINER

1

RAY PRICE

Disclaimer

This book contains information that is solely meant to be educational. Despite their best efforts to present accurate and current information, the author and publisher disclaim all expressed and implied representations and warranties regarding the availability, completeness, accuracy, reliability, suitability, or suitability of the content contained herein for any purpose. The publisher and the author disclaim all responsibility for any loss or harm, including without limitation, consequential or indirect loss or damage, or any loss or damage at all resulting from lost profits or data resulting from using this book.

TABLE OF CONTENTS

INTRODUCTION

Country music has been shaped by many great voices, but few have left a mark as deep and lasting as Ray Price. With a career spanning over six decades, Price was more than just a singer—he was a trailblazer, a risk-taker, and a true artist who refused to be confined to a single sound. From honky tonk barrooms to the grandest stages, his voice carried the soul of country music, constantly evolving yet always staying true to its roots.

This book is a tribute to Ray Price's incredible journey, from his humble beginnings in Texas to his rise as one of the most respected figures in country music. He wasn't just a performer; he was a visionary who changed the course of country music—not once, but multiple times. He started with the raw, twangy honky tonk sound, then transformed it into something smoother and more polished, pioneering what became known as the "Nashville Sound" or "Countrypolitan" style. Some called him a rebel for embracing change, but Price wasn't interested in labels—he simply made the kind of music he believed in.

For many fans, Price will always be the man who gave us "Crazy Arms," a song that became one of the biggest country hits of its time. But his legacy goes far beyond one song. Over the years, he continued to push boundaries with classics like "Heartaches by the Number," "Night Life," and the unforgettable "For the Good Times." His voice, rich and powerful, could convey heartbreak and hope with equal force. Whether backed by a simple steel guitar or a full orchestra, his singing was always pure, always honest.

But Ray Price was more than just his music. He was a mentor to future legends, a bandleader who helped launch the careers of artists like Willie Nelson and Roger Miller. He was a fighter, too—battling industry expectations, health struggles, and personal hardships, yet always emerging with grace and dignity. Even in his later years, when many artists step away from the spotlight, Price continued to record, perform, and share his love of music with the world.

In this book, we'll explore the many chapters of Ray Price's life, from his early days in rural Texas to his rise in Nashville, his bold musical shifts, and his lasting impact on the genre. We'll look at the friendships, the rivalries, the

RAY PRICE

triumphs, and the challenges that shaped him. Most importantly, we'll see how his music continues to live on, inspiring new generations of country artists and fans.

Ray Price may have left this world, but his voice, his songs, and his influence remain as strong as ever. This is the story of a man who never stopped evolving, never stopped singing, and never stopped believing in the power of music. His legacy is not just in the records he made but in the way his music continues to touch hearts today.

So, whether you're a longtime fan or just discovering his work, let's take a journey through the life and career of Ray Price—a country legend whose music will never fade.

CHAPTER 1: THE EARLY YEARS – RAY PRICE'S ROOTS: A CHEROKEE COWBOY'S BEGINNINGS

Ray Price was born on January 12, 1926, in Perryville, Texas, a small rural community where life was simple but tough. He grew up during the Great Depression, a time when families struggled to make ends meet, and hard work was not an option but a necessity. His father, Walter Clifton Price, was a farmer, and his mother, Clara Bradley Price, was a homemaker. When Ray was just a young boy, his parents divorced, which was not as common in those days, and he ended up living with his mother.

One of the most significant influences in Ray Price's heritage was his Native American ancestry. He was part Cherokee, a fact that he acknowledged throughout his life. His identity as a Cherokee cowboy was not just a label—it was a way of life. Growing up in the rugged landscapes of Texas, he was surrounded by cowboys, ranchers, and hardworking folks who lived off the land. The values of resilience, determination, and self-reliance were ingrained in him from an early age. These qualities would later define his career as he navigated the often unforgiving world of the music industry.

Music was always present in Ray Price's early years, but it was not his only interest. Like many boys in Texas, he spent a great deal of time riding horses, helping out on farms, and learning the ways of the cowboy lifestyle. However, he was also fascinated by the radio, which brought the sounds of country, gospel, and Western swing into his home. The voices of Jimmie Rodgers, Bob Wills, and Ernest Tubb filled the airwaves, leaving a lasting impression on the young Price.

During his teenage years, Ray attended high school in Dallas, where he continued to develop a love for music. Although he didn't come from a particularly musical family, he found himself drawn to singing and playing the guitar. Like many country artists of his time, he wasn't formally trained in music; he learned by listening, imitating, and feeling the rhythm of the songs that played on the radio.

His upbringing in Texas, combined with his Cherokee roots and cowboy lifestyle, shaped the man he would become. He wasn't just another aspiring musician; he was a product of his environment, carrying the spirit of Texas and the traditions of country music with him. He had no idea that one day he would become one of the greatest voices in country music history.

Growing Up in Texas: Influences and Inspirations

Ray Price's childhood in Texas was shaped by more than just the hard work of ranch life—it was also filled with the rich sounds of country and Western music. At the time, the Texas music scene was thriving, with honky tonk bars, dance halls, and barn dances serving as the lifeblood of the community.

One of Price's earliest musical influences was Jimmie Rodgers, often called "The Father of Country Music." Rodgers' distinctive yodeling and storytelling style captivated young Price, who admired how the singer blended blues, folk, and country into a sound that felt raw and authentic. Another key influence was Bob Wills, the king of Western swing, whose upbeat, danceable music was a staple at Texas honky tonks.

But it wasn't just professional musicians who shaped Ray Price's love for music. Growing up in a working-class community, he was surrounded by local musicians who played at family gatherings, church services, and town events. The blend of gospel, blues, and traditional country music became part of his identity. As he got older, he began performing informally, singing at local events and playing guitar whenever he had the chance.

Despite his growing passion for music, Ray Price's early years were not entirely focused on becoming a musician. After high school, he attended North Texas Agricultural College (now the University of Texas at Arlington), where he studied veterinary medicine. At the time, he wasn't thinking about a music career—he saw himself working with animals, something he had always enjoyed. However, life had other plans for him.

His college years were interrupted by World War II. Like many young men of his generation, Ray Price answered the call to serve his country. He joined the United States Marine Corps and was stationed in the Pacific during the later years of the war. While his time in the military took him away from music, it also instilled in him a sense of discipline and perseverance that would serve him well in his future career.

After the war ended, Ray returned to Texas and faced a crossroads in his life. He could continue his studies and become a veterinarian, or he could pursue his growing love for music. Deep down, he knew that music was his true calling. Encouraged by friends and fellow musicians, he began performing more seriously, and soon, he realized that his voice had something special—something that could take him far beyond the small towns of Texas.

First Steps into Country Music

The transition from singing at local events to becoming a professional musician was not easy, but Ray Price was determined to make it happen. In the late 1940s, he started performing on local radio stations, which was one of the best ways for aspiring musicians to get noticed at the time. Stations like KRLD in Dallas and KXLA in Fort Worth gave him the opportunity to sing live, reaching an audience far beyond his immediate community.

One of his first big breaks came when he landed a spot on the legendary *Big D Jamboree*, a popular country music show broadcast out of Dallas. The show was a proving ground for many young artists, and it put him in front of larger audiences. Performing alongside established country stars gave him exposure and confidence, and he quickly gained a reputation as a talented and versatile singer.

During this time, Ray Price developed his signature baritone voice—a smooth, commanding sound that set him apart from other singers. He wasn't just another honky tonk performer; his voice had a richness and depth that made people stop and listen. He knew that if he wanted to make it big, he had to get to Nashville, the heart of country music.

In the early 1950s, Ray Price made the move to Nashville, where he hoped to break into the industry. It was a challenging time. The city was full of aspiring musicians, and the competition was fierce. Price struggled to find steady work, taking whatever gigs he could to support himself. He played in bars, honky tonks, and small venues, hoping for a chance to be discovered.

His big moment finally came when he met legendary country singer Hank Williams. The meeting was life-changing—Hank took a liking to Ray and introduced him to key figures in the industry. Williams saw something special in Price, and before long, he was helping him get recording opportunities and performance gigs.

With Hank Williams as a mentor, Ray Price's career began to take off. He signed his first recording contract and started to make a name for himself. His early singles were well-received, but it wasn't until he formed his own band, The Cherokee Cowboys, that he truly found his musical identity.

The road ahead was still uncertain, but one thing was clear—Ray Price was on his way to becoming a country music star. The honky tonk revolution was about to begin, and Price would be at the center of it all.

CHAPTER 2: BREAKING INTO THE MUSIC INDUSTRY – NASHVILLE DREAMS: EARLY STRUGGLES AND TRIUMPHS

By the early 1950s, Ray Price had set his sights on Nashville, the undisputed capital of country music. The city was the heart of the industry, where aspiring musicians came with dreams of making it big. However, breaking into the music business was no easy task. At the time, Nashville was dominated by established artists, powerful record labels, and an industry that was hesitant to take chances on new voices. For Ray Price, the road to stardom was filled with struggles, but he was determined to prove himself.

Upon arriving in Nashville, Price faced the same challenges as many young singers. He had a strong, rich voice, but he needed the right connections to get his foot in the door. He performed wherever he could—small clubs, honky tonks, and local radio stations—hoping to attract attention. Nashville was filled with talent, and competition was fierce. Price knew that if he wanted to stand out, he had to be persistent and patient.

One of his first big breaks came when he landed a spot on the **Grand Ole Opry**, the legendary country music radio show that had launched the careers of countless artists. Being on the Opry was a dream come true, but it was also a test. The audience expected the best, and performing on that stage meant proving that he belonged among the greats. His smooth yet powerful baritone voice quickly caught the attention of industry insiders, and it wasn't long before people began to take notice.

Even with the exposure from the Opry, Ray Price still needed a record deal to truly establish himself as an artist. He eventually signed with **Columbia Records**, a major label that had a long history in country music. This was a huge milestone, as it gave him the opportunity to record and release his music to a nationwide audience. However, the real challenge was finding the right songs and sound that would set him apart.

His early recordings showed promise, but they didn't immediately turn him into a star. Like many artists, Price had to experiment with different styles, trying to find what worked best for him. He was heavily influenced by honky tonk music, a rowdy and emotional style that dominated country radio at the time. But he also had a voice that could handle smooth ballads, a trait that would later play a key role in his career.

Despite the struggles, Ray Price never gave up. He continued to refine his style, work on his stage presence, and build relationships in the industry. His persistence would soon pay off in ways he never expected.

Meeting Hank Williams: A Life-Changing Friendship

One of the most significant turning points in Ray Price's career came when he met **Hank Williams**, one of the biggest stars in country music at the time. Williams was already a legend, known for his heartfelt songwriting, emotional performances, and troubled personal life. Meeting him would change Price's life forever.

Hank Williams saw something special in Ray Price. He recognized the potential in the young singer and took him under his wing. The two quickly formed a close bond, and Williams began mentoring Price, teaching him about the music business, songwriting, and stage performance.

Williams' influence on Price was profound. He encouraged him to embrace the raw emotion of country music, to connect with audiences through storytelling, and to stay true to himself. Price absorbed everything he could, learning not just about singing but also about what it meant to be an artist.

Their friendship went beyond just music. Williams introduced Price to key figures in the industry, helping him make connections that would be crucial for his career. He also gave Price the opportunity to tour with him, opening shows and getting firsthand experience performing for large audiences.

Tragically, Hank Williams' life was cut short when he passed away on January 1, 1953, at the age of 29. His death shocked the country music world, and for Ray Price, it was a heartbreaking loss. However, Williams left behind a legacy that would live on through the artists he influenced, including Price.

In the wake of Williams' passing, Ray Price was given an incredible opportunity—he was asked to take over **Hank's Drifting Cowboys**, the late singer's backing band. This was both an honor and a challenge. Williams had left behind big shoes to fill, and Price knew that stepping into that role would come with high expectations. However, instead of trying to imitate Williams, he used the opportunity to develop his own identity as an artist.

Price's time with the Drifting Cowboys helped him gain more recognition, but he knew that to truly succeed, he needed his own band, his own sound, and his own place in country music history.

The Formation of the Cherokee Cowboys

After gaining experience with Hank Williams' band, Ray Price decided it was time to form his own group. In the mid-1950s, he assembled **The Cherokee Cowboys**, a band that would become one of the most important groups in country music history.

The Cherokee Cowboys were not just a backing band—they were a launching pad for some of the biggest names in country music. Over the years, the group would include future legends such as **Willie Nelson, Roger Miller, Johnny Paycheck, and Buddy Emmons**. Many of these musicians would go on to have successful solo careers, but they got their start playing with Ray Price.

Price had a clear vision for the Cherokee Cowboys. He wanted a band that could deliver the raw, emotional power of honky tonk music while also being versatile enough to experiment with different styles. He handpicked musicians who shared his passion and dedication, and together, they developed a sound that would define an era.

With the Cherokee Cowboys backing him, Price began to record and perform with a newfound confidence. In 1956, he released **"Crazy Arms"**, the song that would change everything. It became his first major hit, spending an incredible **20 weeks at No. 1** on the country charts. The success of "Crazy Arms" established Price as a star and proved that he had found his own voice.

The song also marked the beginning of **The Honky Tonk Revolution**, a movement in country music that emphasized raw emotion, twangy instrumentation, and an energetic rhythm. Ray Price was at the forefront of this movement, leading the charge with his powerful vocals and driving beat.

The success of "Crazy Arms" led to more hits, including **"My Shoes Keep Walking Back to You," "City Lights," and "Heartaches by the Number."** With each new song, Price solidified his place in country music history.

But while he had made it as a honky tonk star, Ray Price was never one to stay in one place for too long. Just as he had shaken up country music with his honky tonk sound, he was about to change it again—this time with a smoother, more sophisticated style that would challenge traditionalists and redefine the genre.

CHAPTER 3: THE HONKY TONK REVOLUTION – DEFINING THE HONKY TONK SOUND

By the mid-1950s, country music was undergoing a transformation, and Ray Price was at the center of it. While the genre had always embraced themes of heartbreak, loneliness, and hard living, the honky tonk sound took these emotions and amplified them with driving rhythms, twangy steel guitars, and a vocal delivery that could cut straight to the heart. Honky tonk music wasn't just something you listened to—it was something you felt.

Ray Price didn't invent honky tonk, but he played a massive role in defining and popularizing its signature sound. Before he arrived on the scene, honky tonk songs were often slower, more subdued, and featured a laid-back rhythm. Price changed that by introducing a new type of beat—what became known as the "Ray Price Shuffle." This rhythmic shuffle featured a steady 4/4 beat with a strong walking bass line, crisp drumming, and a swing-like groove that made his music instantly recognizable.

This shuffle beat was revolutionary. It took traditional country music and gave it an energy that was perfect for the dance halls and honky tonk bars where people gathered to drink, dance, and forget their troubles.

Price's music was emotional, yet it had a rhythm that made people want to move.

The key ingredients of the Ray Price honky tonk sound included:

- **A Driving Bass Line: Instead of the slow, plodding beats of earlier country ballads, Price's music had a rhythm that kept the song moving forward.**
- **Crisp Drumming: The drum patterns in Price's songs were more prominent than in previous country recordings, adding to the infectious shuffle feel.**
- **Steel Guitar & Fiddle: The twang of the steel guitar and the wail of the fiddle were essential elements that kept his music deeply rooted in country tradition.**

- **Strong, Clear Vocals: Price's baritone voice was rich and commanding, making every lyric hit home.**

This new approach to honky tonk music set Price apart from his peers. While other artists were sticking to the old formulas, he was pushing the boundaries, blending traditional country sounds with a livelier, more polished energy.

"Crazy Arms" and the Breakthrough Moment

While Ray Price had been working hard to build his career, his true breakthrough came in 1956 with the release of "Crazy Arms." Up until that point, he had been gaining recognition, but he hadn't had that one song that catapulted him to national stardom. "Crazy Arms" changed everything.

33

The song was a massive success, spending an unprecedented 20 weeks at No. 1 on the Billboard country charts. It wasn't just a hit—it was a game-changer. It introduced the Ray Price Shuffle to the world and solidified his place as one of the top artists in country music.

So, what made "Crazy Arms" such a defining song?

- **Emotional Depth: The song told a tale of heartbreak and longing, a theme that resonated with country music fans. The lyrics captured the pain of lost love, something almost everyone could relate to.**
- **Unique Sound: The shuffle beat made the song stand out from other country**

hits of the time. It had a rhythm that made it impossible to ignore.

- Price's Vocal Performance: His deep, controlled voice brought out every ounce of emotion in the lyrics. Unlike the high, nasal tones of many earlier country singers, Price's baritone voice was smooth and commanding, drawing listeners in.

The success of "Crazy Arms" opened the floodgates for Ray Price. With one song, he had proven that he was not just another honky tonk singer—he was a force to be reckoned with. It also cemented his reputation as a leader in the honky tonk revolution.

Following "Crazy Arms," Price continued to release a string of hits, including:

- **"My Shoes Keep Walking Back to You" (1957)**
- **"City Lights" (1958)**
- **"Heartaches by the Number" (1959)**

Each of these songs built upon the honky tonk sound that Price had helped define. He was on top of the world, dominating the charts and influencing a new wave of country musicians.

The Impact on Traditional Country

Ray Price's honky tonk revolution didn't just change his own career—it changed country music as a whole. His introduction of the shuffle beat and his polished yet emotional sound pushed the genre into new territory.However, not everyone was on board with these changes. Traditionalists within the

industry saw Price's style as a departure from the raw, stripped-down sound of early country music. Some critics believed that his music was too polished, too rhythmic, and too influenced by Western swing.Despite these criticisms, Price's influence couldn't be denied. The honky tonk style that he championed became the dominant sound of country music for years to come. His innovations inspired countless other artists, and the shuffle beat he popularized became a staple of the genre.Artists such as George Jones, Merle Haggard, and Buck Owens took cues from Price's honky tonk style and incorporated elements of it into their own music. Even in later years, when country music evolved into new styles, the influence of Ray Price's honky tonk sound remained.By the end of the 1950s, Ray Price had firmly established himself as a country music icon. He had revolutionized the honky tonk style, created a new rhythmic sound, and set the stage for the next phase of his career. But Price was never content to stay in one place musically. Just as he had changed country music with the honky tonk revolution, he was about to shake things up again—this time with a sound that would redefine what country music could be.

CHAPTER 4: THE COUNTRYPOLITAN SHIFT – A NEW SOUND: STRINGS, ORCHESTRAS, AND SMOOTH VOCALS

By the early 1960s, country music was once again undergoing a transformation, and Ray Price was at the forefront of it. While honky tonk had been the dominant sound of the previous decade, a new style was beginning to emerge—one that was smoother, more polished, and aimed at a broader audience. This new sound, later called "Countrypolitan," blended traditional country elements with lush orchestration, background vocals, and a more refined production style.

Ray Price had already proven himself as a master of honky tonk, but he was never one to be confined to a single style. As the music industry evolved, so did his approach. While many country artists resisted change, fearing that straying too far from tradition would alienate their fan base, Price embraced it. He saw an opportunity to expand country music's reach by introducing elements that could appeal to both country fans and a mainstream audience.

This transition wasn't immediate. It began gradually, with Price experimenting with smoother arrangements and more sophisticated instrumentation in his recordings. Instead of relying solely on fiddles and steel guitars, he started incorporating string sections, orchestras, and backup choirs. His voice, already powerful and commanding, became even more controlled and refined, perfectly suited for the more polished sound he was creating.

The countrypolitan style aimed to bridge the gap between country and pop music, making country music more accessible to a wider audience. Unlike the raw, barroom-ready energy of honky tonk, countrypolitan songs were carefully arranged and produced, often featuring gentler tempos and lush harmonies. Some fans of traditional country music were skeptical, believing that this new style was too polished and lacked the grit of classic country. But for Ray Price, the transition was not about abandoning his roots—it was about expanding what country music could be.

"For the Good Times" and the Reinvention of Country

Ray Price's bold shift in musical style culminated in one of the biggest hits of his career—"For the Good Times" (1970). Written by Kris Kristofferson, the song was a slow, emotional ballad that showcased a softer, more sentimental side of Price. It was dramatically different from the honky tonk songs that had made him famous, featuring gentle strings, a smooth melody, and an introspective, heartfelt vocal performance.

"For the Good Times" became a massive success, reaching No. 1 on the country charts and crossing over to the pop charts. The song

won a Grammy Award for Best Country Male Vocal Performance and introduced Ray Price to an entirely new audience. With this song, he had successfully bridged the gap between country and pop, proving that country music could be just as elegant and emotionally powerful as any mainstream ballad.

The impact of "For the Good Times" went beyond just being a hit song. It cemented Price's reputation as a musical innovator. He had taken a risk by moving away from honky tonk, and it had paid off in a big way. He followed up with other countrypolitan hits, including:

- "I Won't Mention It Again" (1971)
- "She's Got to Be a Saint" (1972)
- "You're the Best Thing That Ever Happened to Me" (1973)

Each of these songs continued the countrypolitan sound, further establishing Ray Price as a pioneer of the genre.

Fan Reactions: Traditionalists vs. Modernists

While Ray Price's transition into countrypolitan music brought him new success, it also sparked controversy within the country music community. Traditionalists, who had loved his honky tonk sound, were not all happy with the change. Some felt that he had "sold out" by embracing a more polished, pop-influenced style.

Many hardcore country fans missed the twang of the steel guitar, the shuffle beats, and the honky tonk energy that had defined Price's earlier work. To them, the lush orchestration and smooth ballads felt like a departure from real country music. Price himself acknowledged these criticisms but was unapologetic about his evolution. He believed that music should grow and change, and he refused to be confined to a single style.

Despite the skepticism from some country purists, Price's influence continued to grow. His embrace of countrypolitan music helped bring new listeners to country music, broadening its appeal. While some of his longtime fans may have resisted the change, many others embraced it, and Price gained an entirely new audience that might never have listened to country music otherwise.

The countrypolitan era of country music would go on to inspire future artists like Kenny Rogers, Glen Campbell, and Ronnie Milsap, who would continue blending country and pop to great success in the 1970s and beyond.

Ray Price's ability to reinvent himself without losing the essence of who he was set him apart from many of his peers. While other artists struggled to adapt to changing musical trends, Price thrived, proving that country music could evolve without losing its soul.

A Lasting Impact

Looking back, Ray Price's transition to the countrypolitan sound was one of the most important moments in his career. It showed his fearlessness as an artist, his willingness to take risks, and his ability to shape the direction of country music.

Even today, "For the Good Times" remains one of the greatest country songs of all time, a testament to the power of emotionally driven storytelling and timeless melodies.

Ray Price had revolutionized honky tonk in the 1950s, and by the 1970s, he had done the same for countrypolitan music. Few artists could claim to have been at the forefront of two major country music revolutions, but Ray Price did just that.His legacy as both a honky tonk pioneer and a countrypolitan trailblazer ensures that his music continues to resonate with audiences of all generations. While some fans may always prefer one era of his career over the other, the truth is that Ray Price's greatest strength was his ability to evolve, adapt, and remain true to his artistry.As country music moved forward, Price's influence could be felt in both traditional and modern country artists alike. His willingness

to embrace change while maintaining the emotional depth of country music made him one of the most respected figures in the genre's history.

CHAPTER 5: COLLABORATIONS AND INFLUENCE – WORKING WITH LEGENDS: WILLIE NELSON, MERLE HAGGARD, AND MORE

Ray Price was not just a solo star—he was a collaborator, mentor, and friend to some of the most influential artists in country music. His career spanned multiple generations, and along the way, he worked with legendary figures such as Willie Nelson, Merle Haggard, Johnny Cash, and Waylon Jennings. These collaborations weren't just about recording songs together; they were about shaping the sound of country music and passing down its traditions.

One of the most significant partnerships of Price's career was with Willie Nelson. In the 1970s, when Nelson was breaking away from the rigid structures of Nashville to forge his own path in the outlaw country movement, Price remained a strong supporter. Their collaborations blended traditional country with a more relaxed, narrative-driven style.

One of their most well-known projects together was "San Antonio Rose" (1980), an album of classic country covers that paid tribute to Bob Wills, one of their mutual influences. The album highlighted their deep respect for the roots of country music while also showcasing their ability to bring a fresh perspective to timeless songs.

Similarly, Price's work with Merle Haggard was built on mutual admiration and a shared love for traditional country sounds. Haggard, who idolized Price's honky tonk roots, often cited him as a major influence. They recorded several songs together, blending Haggard's Bakersfield sound with Price's smooth vocals and honky tonk rhythms.

Through these collaborations, Price demonstrated his willingness to embrace both tradition and innovation. Whether he was working with classic country artists or newer voices, he never let ego stand in the way of great music. He understood that country music was a shared art form, one that thrived when artists worked together to keep it evolving.

The Cherokee Cowboys: Launching Other Stars' Careers

Ray Price was more than just a singer—he was a talent scout, mentor, and bandleader. His backing band, The Cherokee Cowboys, became a training ground for some of the biggest names in country music. Many artists who played in Price's band went on to have legendary careers of their own.

Some of the most notable musicians who got their start with The Cherokee Cowboys include:

51

- **Willie Nelson – Before becoming a country icon, Nelson was a bass player in Price's band. It was during this time that Nelson wrote some of his early classics, including "Night Life," which Price recorded and turned into a hit.**
- **Roger Miller – Best known for songs like "King of the Road," Miller was another young musician who cut his teeth as a member of The Cherokee Cowboys. His time with Price helped him refine his songwriting and performing skills.**
- **Johnny Bush – Known for his hit "Whiskey River," Bush was also part of The Cherokee Cowboys before making it big on his own.**
- **Buddy Emmons – A legendary steel guitarist, Emmons played a crucial role**

in shaping Price's signature honky tonk sound before becoming one of the most respected musicians in country music history.

Price didn't just hire talented musicians—he nurtured them, encouraged them, and gave them the platform they needed to develop their own careers. He had an incredible eye for talent and was never threatened by the idea of his band members outgrowing their roles. Instead, he saw it as his duty to help shape the next generation of country stars.

Influence on Future Generations of Country Artists

Ray Price's impact on country music didn't stop with the artists he collaborated with or mentored directly. His influence extended far beyond his immediate circle, shaping the sound and direction of country music for decades to come.

His honky tonk shuffle and rich baritone vocals became a template for countless country artists who followed in his footsteps. Artists such as George Strait, Alan Jackson, Randy Travis, and Dwight Yoakam all drew inspiration from Price's blend of traditional country and modern innovation.

In fact, many of Price's stylistic choices—his ability to transition between honky tonk and countrypolitan, his deep emotional delivery, and his commitment to storytelling—became fundamental elements of country music itself.

- George Strait, one of the most successful country artists of all time,

has often cited Ray Price as a key
influence, particularly in how he
blended traditional country with a
more polished, radio-friendly sound.

- Randy Travis followed a similar path,
  embracing both the emotional depth of
  Price's ballads and the honky tonk
  energy of his earlier work.

- Garth Brooks also drew from Price's
  ability to push country music beyond its
  traditional boundaries while still
  honoring its roots.

Even in modern country music, traces of Ray
Price's influence can be heard. Artists like
Chris Stapleton, Cody Johnson, and Sturgill
Simpson continue to channel the raw,
emotional power that Price brought to his
music.

A Legacy That Lives On

Ray Price's influence is immeasurable. He wasn't just another country singer—he was a bridge between generations, a mentor to legends, and a pioneer who reshaped the sound of country music multiple times.

His legacy is heard in the voices of today's country singers, in the shuffle beat that still dominates honky tonk dance halls, and in the classic ballads that continue to touch listeners decades after they were first recorded.

Perhaps the greatest testament to Price's influence is the lasting love and respect he receives from fans and fellow musicians alike. Even after his passing, his music remains a vital part of country history, a reminder that true artistry never fades.

RAY PRICE

CHAPTER 6: CHALLENGES AND COMEBACKS – THE CHANGING COUNTRY MUSIC SCENE

By the late 1970s and early 1980s, country music was going through another transformation. The traditional honky tonk and countrypolitan sounds that Ray Price had helped define were being replaced by a slicker, more commercialized version of country music. Pop influences were becoming stronger, and a younger generation of artists was taking over the airwaves.

While some country legends adapted to these changes, others struggled to find their place.

Ray Price, having already reinvented himself multiple times throughout his career, now faced the challenge of staying relevant in a music industry that was moving away from his signature sound.

As the Urban Cowboy movement took over the country music scene in the early 1980s, emphasizing polished production and crossover appeal, Price found himself at a crossroads. He was a country music giant, but the industry was prioritizing a younger, more radio-friendly sound. However, rather than conform to trends, Price stayed true to his artistic vision.

Despite the shifts in the industry, Price remained steadfast in his commitment to high-quality music, refusing to release songs that didn't align with his artistic values. This commitment kept his core fan base loyal, even if mainstream radio played him less frequently.

Battling Personal and Professional Struggles

While Price was dealing with challenges in the industry, he also faced personal struggles, including financial difficulties and health issues. Like many artists who had been in the business for decades, he experienced periods where record sales declined, and securing a record deal became more difficult.

The pressures of a long career, combined with the ups and downs of the music business, led to moments of self-doubt and frustration. However, Price never allowed these struggles to break him. Instead, he used them as motivation to continue making music on his own terms.

During this period, Price also faced health issues that made performing more difficult. While he had always been known for his powerful voice and commanding stage presence, age and illness began to take a toll. Yet, Price remained determined to continue sharing his music with the world.

Rediscovering His Audience

Although mainstream country music had shifted toward a younger, more pop-influenced sound, there was still a large audience of traditional country fans who longed for the classic sounds of honky tonk and countrypolitan. In the late 1980s and early 1990s, a traditional country revival began, led by artists like George Strait, Alan Jackson, and Randy Travis—many of whom had been inspired by Price himself.

Seeing this renewed appreciation for traditional country, Price took the opportunity to reconnect with audiences who had always loved his music. He continued touring, performing for loyal fans who still cherished his signature sound.

During this time, Price also found new ways to share his music. He embraced independent record labels that allowed him more creative freedom, rather than relying on major Nashville labels that were focused on younger artists. This move proved to be successful, as it allowed him to record music that stayed true to his legacy without the pressure of conforming to industry trends.

Additionally, Price's collaborations with younger artists and fellow country legends helped introduce his music to new generations. By working with artists who respected and admired his contributions, he remained an active and influential figure in country music, even as the industry continued to change.

A True Country Music Fighter

Ray Price's journey through the ever-changing country music industry was not always easy, but it was always driven by passion, resilience, and a deep love for the art of storytelling. Despite the challenges he faced—whether from shifting industry trends, personal struggles, or health issues—he never lost his determination to create meaningful music.

Unlike many artists who faded into obscurity when the industry changed, Price fought to keep traditional country music alive. His ability to adapt, reinvent himself, and remain true to his roots allowed him to have one of the longest and most respected careers in country music history.

His story is one of persistence, courage, and an unbreakable connection to his fans. No matter what obstacles came his way, he always found a way to come back stronger—proving that true legends never fade.

CHAPTER 7: THE FINAL YEARS AND FAREWELL TOUR – A LIFETIME OF MUSIC: STILL PERFORMING IN HIS 80S

Even in his later years, Ray Price remained a force in country music. Unlike many of his peers who retired or slowed down, Price never lost his passion for performing. Well into his 80s, he continued to tour, record new music, and connect with his devoted fans. His voice, though aged, remained strong, carrying the same depth and emotion that had defined his career.

Price's ability to perform with the same energy and passion he had in his younger years amazed audiences. Fans who had followed him since his honky tonk days in the 1950s were now attending his concerts with their children and grandchildren, proving the timeless appeal of his music.

Even as mainstream country music moved further toward pop influences, Price's concerts remained packed. He often performed in smaller, intimate venues where he could truly engage with his audience. Whether he was singing honky tonk classics like "Crazy Arms" or his countrypolitan hits like "For the Good Times," fans cherished the opportunity to hear him live.

Despite his advancing age, Price was determined to keep traditional country music alive. He viewed performing as more than just a career—it was his life's purpose. He once said in an interview, "As long as there's a stage and people willing to listen, I'll be singing."

Recording the Final Album: *Beauty Is…*

Even after decades in the music business, Ray Price was not content to simply rest on his past success. In 2013, despite battling serious health issues, he returned to the studio one final time to record his last album, *Beauty Is…*

This album was deeply personal. Rather than focusing on the honky tonk and countrypolitan styles that had defined different eras of his career, *Beauty Is…* was a collection of gentle, heartfelt love songs. The album was a tribute to his wife, Janie, whom he had been married to for over 40 years.

Price's voice on the album was softer, reflecting the toll of time and illness, yet it still carried the unmistakable warmth and sincerity that had made him a legend. The songs, carefully selected and beautifully arranged, served as a final farewell to his fans—a reminder of the emotional depth and storytelling that defined his music.

Though Price knew his time was limited, he put everything he had into this album. It was released in 2014, just months after his passing, and was widely praised by critics and fans alike. Many listeners considered it one of the most touching albums of his career, as it reflected the wisdom, love, and gratitude of a man who had spent a lifetime making music.

Saying Goodbye: His Passing and Tributes

In 2012, Ray Price was diagnosed with pancreatic cancer, one of the most aggressive and difficult-to-treat forms of cancer. Despite the devastating news, he remained strong and continued performing as long as his health allowed.

By late 2013, Price's condition had worsened, and he was hospitalized several times. Even then, he maintained a positive outlook and stayed in touch with fans through public statements, reassuring them that he was at peace with whatever the future held.

On December 16, 2013, Ray Price passed away at the age of 87 at his home in Mount Pleasant, Texas. The country music world mourned the loss of one of its greatest voices.

His passing marked the end of an era, but his music and influence would live on forever.

Tributes poured in from fellow artists, fans, and industry leaders. Willie Nelson, Merle Haggard, George Strait, and many others publicly expressed their admiration for Price, acknowledging the profound impact he had on country music.

At his funeral, friends and family spoke about his warmth, generosity, and passion for music. Many described him as not only a legendary singer but also a kind and humble man who never lost touch with his roots.

His longtime friend Willie Nelson paid tribute by saying, "Ray Price didn't just sing country music—he defined it."

A Legacy That Lives Forever

Ray Price's passing marked the end of a remarkable career, but his music continues to resonate with listeners of all ages. His ability to seamlessly blend honky tonk, countrypolitan, and traditional country made him one of the most versatile and enduring artists in country music history.

His songs remain staples in country music history, and his influence can still be heard in the voices of today's artists. Whether through the classic shuffle beat he popularized, the emotional ballads he perfected, or the generations of musicians he mentored, Ray Price's legacy is woven into the very fabric of country music.

Even today, his songs continue to be played on country radio stations, his albums remain in circulation, and his name is spoken with reverence by artists who followed in his footsteps. His legacy is not just about the hits he recorded but about the heart, soul, and authenticity he brought to every note he sang.

Though he may be gone, Ray Price's music will never fade. His voice, his songs, and his influence will live on for generations to come.

CHAPTER 8: RAY PRICE'S LASTING LEGACY – THE ENDURING APPEAL OF HIS MUSIC

Ray Price's music continues to resonate with audiences across generations. His songs, whether honky tonk anthems or smooth countrypolitan ballads, have stood the test of time. While many artists fade into history, Price's ability to evolve while remaining true to his roots has kept his music relevant and cherished.

His honky tonk hits like "Crazy Arms," "Heartaches by the Number," and "City Lights" still fill dance halls and honky tonk bars, where country fans two-step to the same beats that captivated listeners in the 1950s. Meanwhile, his countrypolitan ballads, especially "For the Good Times" and "Night Life," remain some of the most powerful and emotionally charged recordings in country music history.

Streaming platforms, digital downloads, and reissued albums have introduced new generations to his music. Younger listeners, many of whom were born long after his prime, are discovering his timeless sound—a testament to the depth and authenticity of his artistry.

Price's ability to bridge multiple generations is rare in country music. He was not only a pioneer but also a guiding force that shaped the evolution of the genre.

Honoring Ray Price: Awards, Tributes, and Influence

Ray Price's contributions to country music were recognized with numerous awards and honors throughout his career.

- **He was inducted into the Country Music Hall of Fame in 1996, a well-deserved recognition of his impact on the genre.**
- **He received two Grammy Awards, including one for his classic hit "For the Good Times."**
- **The Academy of Country Music (ACM) and the Country Music Association (CMA) honored him for his influence and innovation in country music.**

Even after his passing, tributes to Ray Price continue to pour in.

- Fellow country legends, including Willie Nelson, George Strait, and Alan Jackson, have paid homage to his musical influence and friendship.
- Modern country artists such as Chris Stapleton and Cody Johnson have cited him as a major influence, incorporating elements of his signature shuffle beat and rich vocal delivery into their own music.
- Tribute concerts and special performances dedicated to Price's music have been held at the Grand Ole Opry, the Ryman Auditorium, and other historic venues.

His hometown of Perryville, Texas, has also taken steps to preserve his legacy, with efforts to honor his contributions through local festivals, museum exhibits, and music events that celebrate his impact on country music.

How His Sound Still Shapes Country Music Today

Ray Price's influence is still alive in modern country music, even as the genre continues to evolve.

- The shuffle beat that Price perfected in his honky tonk days remains a staple in traditional country and can be heard in songs by artists like George Strait, Midland, and The Mavericks.
- His smooth baritone vocals and countrypolitan arrangements paved the

way for singers who bring deep emotion and polished instrumentation into their music.

- His ability to adapt and evolve without losing his artistic identity is something that many artists strive for today.

While mainstream country has shifted toward pop influences, the roots of Ray Price's sound remain strong. Traditional country artists, independent musicians, and fans who appreciate the heart and soul of classic country music continue to honor his contributions.

A Legacy That Will Never Fade

Ray Price was more than just a country singer—he was a musical architect, a trailblazer who helped shape country music across multiple decades. His willingness to embrace change while still honoring tradition made him one of the most respected and enduring figures in the genre.

His legacy is not just about the hits he recorded or the awards he won. It's about the emotion he brought to his music, the artists he inspired, and the fans who continue to cherish his songs.

Even though he has passed on, his music lives forever. Every time someone listens to "For the Good Times", dances to "Crazy Arms", or hears a modern country artist channel his spirit, Ray Price's influence continues.

His story is one of passion, perseverance, and authenticity—qualities that define the very best of country music. His voice may be silent, but his music will never stop playing.

Ray Price's lasting legacy is not just in country music history books. It's in the hearts of the fans, the voices of the singers he inspired, and the timeless songs that will be played for generations to come.

The legend lives on.

CONCLUSION

The Timeless Legacy of Ray Price

Ray Price was more than just a country music star—he was a pioneer, an innovator, and a storyteller whose influence continues to shape the genre long after his passing. His music, spanning from the honky tonk era to the smooth countrypolitan sound, touched the hearts of millions and left an unforgettable mark on country music history.

Few artists have successfully reinvented themselves the way Price did. He not only helped define the classic honky tonk sound with songs like *"Crazy Arms"* but also led country music into the countrypolitan era, proving that traditional music could evolve

81

without losing its soul. His ability to blend deep emotion, rich instrumentation, and timeless storytelling set him apart as one of the greatest vocalists in country music.

But beyond his achievements and awards, Price's true legacy lives in the artists he inspired and the fans who still cherish his music. His influence can be heard in the songs of George Strait, Willie Nelson, Merle Haggard, and even modern traditionalists like Cody Johnson and Chris Stapleton.

Even today, his music remains as powerful and relevant as ever. His songs continue to be played on country radio, streamed online, and performed in dance halls and honky tonks across the world. New generations of country fans continue to discover his voice, proving that great music never dies.

Ray Price's journey—from a small-town Texas boy to a country music legend—was filled with challenges, reinvention, and unwavering dedication to his craft. He was a man who never stopped pushing boundaries, and even in his final years, he remained committed to his music and his fans.

Though he has passed on, his voice still echoes through the country music world. His passion, innovation, and artistry ensure that Ray Price is not just a name in history books but a living, breathing part of country music's DNA.

The shuffle beat, the velvet-smooth vocals, the deep emotional ballads—these will never fade. They will live on in the hearts of those who love true country music.

Ray Price may be gone, but his songs, his influence, and his spirit will never be forgotten. His music is a gift that will continue to touch lives for generations to come.

For the good times—and forever.

Made in the USA
Columbia, SC
31 March 2025

55958909R00048